HAMLYN
Pet Guides

GUINEA PIGS

Isabel Day

Hamlyn

London · New York · Sydney · Toronto

Introduction

Pet guinea pigs or cavies are probably descended from the wild *cui* that the Incas kept 500 years ago. These were smaller than our guinea pigs and were often eaten by the Incas on special occasions. When the Spanish conquistadors landed in South America they noticed that the skinned animals looked like tiny pigs and called them *Cochinillo das Indas* or the 'little Indian pig', and the prefix 'guinea' was probably added from the fact that the Spaniards took them to Guiana before they then spread into Europe as pets, finally arriving in Britain in about 1750. Today many South American Indians still keep them as a source of food and the government in Peru is attempting to breed bigger specimens as an economical meat supply.

The wild South American guinea pigs live in family groups, or colonies, and are a drab pepper and salt colour.

Guinea pigs are rodents, a group of mammals containing over 1700 species. The word rodent comes from the Latin word *rodere* meaning 'to gnaw'. Rats, mice and squirrels are all rodents as are the larger capybaras seen in zoos, which are close relatives of the pet guinea pig. Rodents have special teeth: four incisors shaped like chisels at the front which grow continually and are worn down by gnawing and a set of grinding teeth for chewing that are hidden at the back of the animal's cheeks. Other peculiarities include four toes on the front feet but only three on the back ones, and the absence of a tail, although you can feel an arrow-shaped formation of small bones under the cavy's skin at the base of the spine.

Guinea pigs are very attractive animals; in many ways they are an ideal first pet for a child.

Choosing and buying

First of all, before purchasing a guinea pig, remember that this is a live animal and that it will be your responsibility to care for it every day. A guinea pig cannot be left to fend for itself for a few days while you go on holiday: it must be fed regularly, cleaned out and cared for. It will usually live for four or five years or even longer, so make sure that you are well prepared for your new pet before you go to buy him. To begin with, you will need a sturdy cage, bedding, and food and water.

Probably the best age to buy a guinea pig is when it is about 6-8 weeks old and is independent of its mother. It should weigh about 225-285g (8-10oz) and look well fed. At this age it will adapt well to its new home and soon become very tame.

It does not make a great deal of difference whether you

It is very important that your pet has fresh green food and water every day.

Two guinea pigs of the same sex will live happily in the same hutch if put together at an early age.

buy a male (a boar) or a female (a sow), though boars are slightly bolder. Should you want to keep two guinea pigs they should be the same sex so that they will live happily together. However, they should be both young when introduced as adults may fight each other.

Types of coat You will probably have looked at a number of guinea pigs and will have decided what sort you would like. There are numerous colours and three basic coats: the smooth-coated short-haired, the rosetted

You will find that there is a great variety of different colours and markings amongst guinea pigs; some also have different types of coat, either long, fluffy or smooth. Have a good look around before deciding which you prefer, you may find it difficult to make up your mind!

rough-haired and the long-haired. Of these three coats, the smooth and the rough-haired guinea pigs are the easiest to keep clean and well groomed. Think very hard before choosing a long-haired guinea pig as they need daily brushing and cleaning, in fact it is best to cut their coat regularly to a length that just brushes the floor as this will prevent it from matting and causing the animal distress.

Where to buy There are several places where you can obtain your guinea pig. You may know someone whose pet has had babies, you can go to a pet shop or to a breeder. If you are going to a pet shop then make sure that it is a clean, well-run place with a good reputation and that the animals look alert and healthy. Your guinea pig should be able to run about easily, his eyes should be bright and large and his mouth and nose clean. Make sure that he is not scratching and that his fur is healthy and thick, also that his breathing is even and quiet. It is wise to find out if the pet shop has separated the boars from

the sows whilst they are in the shop, otherwise the chances are that the sows will be pregnant!

The majority of guinea pigs to be found in pet shops are cross-breds or 'mongrels', but there are also about 25 different varieties of pure-bred or 'pedigree' guinea pigs – or cavies as their breeders call them. These are bred for exhibition or showing and can be seen at many local shows around the country. You may prefer a pure-bred guinea pig as your pet in which case there will probably be a breeder in your area who can help you or someone in your local Society (see *Addresses* page 31). The different varieties of guinea pig are described overleaf.

When you go to fetch your new pet, remember to take a reasonably strong cardboard box with you to carry the animal home in. The box should not be so small that it will cramp the guinea pig nor be so large that your pet can rush around in fright and possibly come to some harm. A box measuring roughly 30cm x 20cm (12in x 8in), with holes in the lid so that the guinea pig can breathe, is ideal.

Varieties

Pure-bred guinea pigs can be divided into four groups: the smooth short-haired English Self guinea pigs, smooth short-haired guinea pigs with markings, rough-haired or rosetted guinea pigs and, last but not least, the long-haired guinea pigs.

English Self guinea pigs These are completely one colour, and colour is the most important feature of the English Self cavy; it should be even and go right down to the skin.

However, 'type' is almost equally important. 'Type' refers to the overall shape of the guinea pig. It should have a broad head with a good width between the eyes, a short face with large drooping ears and strong high shoulders.

There are eight different colours of English Self, and

Self guinea pigs are very attractive with their short blunt faces and glossy coats.

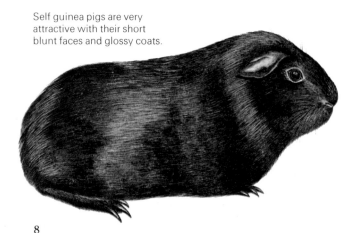

As you can see, the Tortoiseshell and White may be amongst the most beautiful of guinea pigs but it is certainly the hardest to breed to show standard.

probably the most popular is the Self Black. One fault in this guinea pig is an intermixing of red and white hairs, but a well groomed and prepared Black is extremely attractive.

Pink-eyed Whites are also popular. They usually excel in type and should be spotless, though keeping them clean and free from staining is very difficult. There are also Black-eyed Whites but these tend to have grey ears and feet, and are difficult to breed to show standard.

Self Creams are often referred to as the 'champagne cavies'. They usually have very good type and are a beautiful pale cream with dark ruby eyes.

A Himalayan guinea pig. Himalayan babies are born pure white, and the markings do not appear until later.

Self Goldens can vary in colour but should be a rich ginger with pink eyes and should not be confused with the Self Red which is a dark rich mahogany and has black eyes.

The three remaining self guinea pigs are the Self Chocolate, Self Beige and Self Lilac. The Chocolate should be the colour of dark (plain) chocolate with eyes to match, though these have a ruby tinge. The Beige should be a warm pinky beige while the Lilac is a pale even dove grey, again with a pink tinge. Both the Beige and the Lilac have pink eyes.

Smooth, marked guinea pigs All other breeds of guinea pig are known as non-selfs. The smooth, marked varieties include the Agouti, Dutch, Tortoiseshell and White, Roan, Dalmation and Himalayan.

Agoutis are 'ticked' guinea pigs which means that they have bands of two different colours on their hair, giving

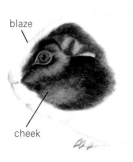

saddle

blaze

cheek

foot stop

A Dutch guinea pig. Many young Dutch guinea pigs do not have the precise show markings necessary to win.

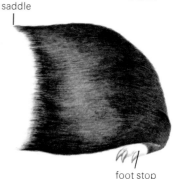

them a speckled look. The three main colours in Agoutis are golden and silver (both with a black base colour), and cinnamon which has a chocolate base colour.

Dutch guinea pigs have the same markings as the Dutch rabbit: the rear half of the animal is coloured with equal white socks on the back feet, and the head markings should be round and even with a blaze of white extending up the middle of the face. They usually have red, chocolate or black markings with a white body colour.

The Tortoiseshell and White guinea pig is often called the 'heartbreak breed', because it is so difficult to breed a show specimen. The ideal 'Tort and White', as it is known in the fancy, is a smooth-coated guinea pig with square and equal patches of black, red and white and with straight demarcation lines down the back and stomach, and adjoining patches of different colours.

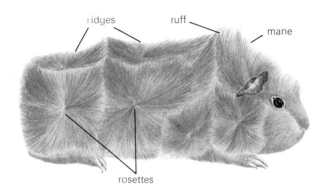

ridges ruff mane

rosettes

An Abyssinian guinea pig. Abyssinians are amongst the most hardy of pure-bred guinea pigs.

Roan guinea pigs have solid-coloured heads and feet, and bodies with an even intermixing of coloured and white hairs.

The Roan should not be confused with the Dalmation. This has a spotted appearance and has Dutch-type head markings.

The Himalayan is marked like a Siamese cat with either a black or light-brown nose and feet (this animal is illustrated on page 10).

Rough-haired guinea pigs These are the Crested and the Abyssinian.

Crested guinea pigs are smooth and short-haired but

what makes them a rough guinea pig is the crest or rosette on their heads above the eyes and below the ears. Crested variations to all the previously mentioned breeds do exist along with the attractive American Crested which has a white crest contrasting with a Self-coloured body. The American Crested, as its name suggests, was the original crested and was imported from Canada in 1972. Whilst it is difficult to breed a good show specimen, it is a very beautiful guinea pig.

Abyssinians are rosetted guinea pigs with a coat about 4cm (1½in) in length. It should have four rosettes in a straight line across the middle and four around the rump with well-defined ridges between them. The coat should, unlike most other breeds, feel harsh to the touch.

Long-haired guinea pigs The Peruvian's hair lies towards its head and therefore falls over its face and sides with a parting down the middle of the back.

The Sheltie and Coronet cavies differ from the Peruvian in that their coats flow backwards leaving the head clear, and in the case of the Coronet the guinea pig has a crest on its head.

All these three have coats that grow continually and are hard to keep clean and tidy unless the hair is regularly trimmed. For show purposes the hair is not cut but is rolled in small paper 'wrappers' each stiffened with a strip of balsa wood and an elastic band to secure it. Show specimens are brushed out every day.

Rare varieties These are varieties of guinea pigs which are mostly relatively new breeds. They cannot be shown extensively yet because of their comparatively short existence, and include the Tortoiseshell, Brindle, Argente and also the Rex with its short, erect, wiry coat.

Housing and equipment

There are many different types of hutches for guinea pigs and before buying your guinea pig make sure that you have a proper home for it. Your guinea pigs will thrive in a well constructed cage in an adequately ventilated shed. Here they will be secure and well protected from the weather and it will be more pleasant for you when you

Your guinea pig's home should be strong, waterproof and easy to clean out.

A heavy food bowl and a
water bottle are essentials.

are looking after them. If you are considering keeping a
number of guinea pigs then a shed with electric light is a
must. However, do make sure that your shed is not
draughty or damp with condensation, and do not use oil
heaters to keep your cavies warm as the fumes are
dangerous to them. For the same reason never keep
guinea pigs in a garage with a car as exhaust fumes are
lethal and will suffocate them.

Should you decide to keep your pet outside you will
need a strong and substantial cage to protect it from bad
weather and possible predators such as foxes, and it
should be raised off the ground for the same reasons.

Your basic cage should be at least 46cm (18in) square
and twice this size for a pair or a sow with a litter,
although of course the height would still be 46cm (18in).
Hutches are best made of wood with fronts that open
completely for easy cleaning, and with a removable litter
board about 8cm (3in) deep across the front so that your
guinea pig won't fall out when you open the door.

If your pet is going to live outdoors it is best for the
cage to have a separate sheltered 'bedroom' compartment
with an opening into the main hutch, this will ensure that

If you are keeping several guinea pigs in a shed, then a tiered system of cages is best.

there is warmth in winter and shade in summer. The top, sides and back should be covered with roofing felt to make the hutch waterproof and it is best if the roof overhangs, giving the guinea pig and yourself more protection in bad weather. In extremely bad weather, cover the wire front loosely with a sack to give your pet more protection from draughts and the damp, or perhaps bring him indoors temporarily.

If you have a lawn which is not fouled by dogs and which you do not treat with weedkiller or fertilizer, you might like to have a run for your guinea pig. This must keep him in and keep cats and dogs out and must have some cover from the sun or a sudden shower of rain, and it is wise for security to have a wire netting bottom to it as well as to the top and sides.

Your guinea pig will require a few other things as well as his hutch. He will need a feeding bowl for his dry food (a heavy one is best as guinea pigs tend to tip them over) and he will need a water bottle which is attached to the wire netting with the nozzle poking through to the guinea pig. This must be kept filled at all times. The guinea pig will need bedding in the hutch to keep warm and dry, ideal bedding is a layer of newspaper covered with about 5cm (2in) of clean woodshavings. (Woodshavings are much better than sawdust which will get in the guinea pig's eyes and can also cause breathing problems.) Finish off the hutch with three or four handfuls of quality hay and remember to top this up every day as your guinea pig will eat it as well as bed on it.

Cages need to be thoroughly cleaned out at least once a week, unless it is very cold when you can top up the cage with shavings and hay to keep your guinea pig warmer. However, a major clean out at regular intervals is absolutely essential for the well being of your guinea pig and you will find that his cage will need a thorough scrubbing out with a mild disinfectant three or four times a year. Make sure that the cage is completely dry before you return your guinea pig to his home as a damp cage is a sure recipe for pneumonia.

Feeding

When you buy your guinea pig ask what food the animal is used to, then you can change the diet gradually so as not to upset your pet. Two meals a day are sufficient, but feed your guinea pigs at regular times as they are creatures of habit and dislike change.

The five essentials in your pet's diet are: dry guinea pig mix or crushed oats, greens and roots, hay and water.

Whether you feed a specially prepared mix or just crushed oats, a good handful (about 42g/1½oz) a day should be plenty for each animal, but if yours is eating every scrap by all means top up the dish.

Guinea pigs, along with monkeys and human beings, are the only creatures which need vitamin C in their food. Consequently it is vitally important that guinea pigs should have daily green food of the highest quality; if you would not be prepared to eat it yourself, then don't expect your pet to! Yellowed greens, potato peelings, etc. are a sure way to health problems. You cannot overfeed your guinea pig: if he's eating it all then you're not giving him enough.

Carrots, chopped raw beetroot, cabbage, swedes, apples, cucumber and cauliflower are all valuable

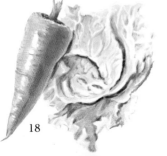

foodstuffs as are fresh grass and dandelion leaves if they are free from any pesticides or chemicals. Remember that many plants such as bindweed, buttercup, foxglove, rhubarb and potato leaves are poisonous.

Good quality hay should be given every day, it is far better than straw and your guinea pig will not thrive without it. A good handful should be sufficient, and any uneaten hay will be used for bedding.

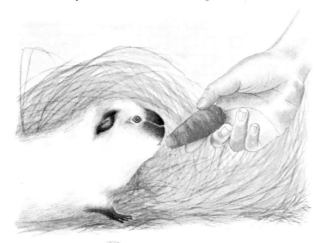

Your guinea pig will enjoy most fresh vegetables and will appreciate a change from day to day. If you feed him titbits, he will soon become tame and watch for your arrival with his meal.

Handling and general care

Handling When you first take your pet home he may well be rather nervous as he may not have been handled very much, and the journey and change of home may frighten him a little. Gradually handle him a little more each day and you will be surprised at how quickly he will become tame and learn to recognize your voice, coming to the bars for a titbit. The best way to pick up your guinea pig is to slide your hand under his body while the other hand is placed on his shoulders to steady him, and then to lift him up gently, making sure that he is secure. Never squeeze your pet or grab him around the middle as this can easily cause internal damage, and never ever pick him up by the scruff of the neck. If you always handle him gently and make sure that other people do the same he will soon be confident and friendly.

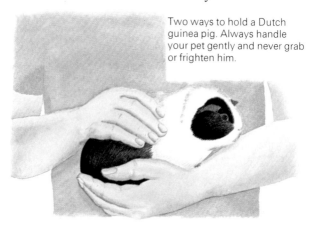

Two ways to hold a Dutch guinea pig. Always handle your pet gently and never grab or frighten him.

Grooming Your guinea pig should not really need bathing unless you intend to show him as he will keep himself very clean, but you can help by brushing the coat regularly with a small brush such as a baby brush, especially if your pet is long-coated. If you should need to bath your pet, use an ordinary mild shampoo and warm water and rinse him well. Make sure he is thoroughly dry either by towelling or by using a hair dryer before you put him back in his hutch, as he could easily catch a chill.

You may notice small white lice moving in your guinea pig's coat; these will not hurt your guinea pig and will probably have arrived in the hay, but your pet will feel more comfortable if you get a special spray or dusting powder from a reputable pet shop to get rid of them.

Nails You will find that as your guinea pig gets older he may need to have his nails cut. These should not need

Your pet will appreciate a
gentle brush sometimes.

trimming until he is at least a year old, but if they do need
some attention you must be very careful because there
will be a lot of bleeding if you cut the vein that runs
down the claw. If the nail is pale in colour it will be much
easier to cut as the vein will be clearly visible, but don't
be tempted to cut the nails too short, particularly the rear
ones.

Teeth Occasionally your guinea pig may have problems
with his teeth, although this is rare. They should be
checked regularly to make sure that they are not
overgrowing and preventing the animal from eating, and
if they do need clipping your vet is the best person to do

it. Should your guinea pig accidentally fall from his cage or from any height, do check the teeth as they may have been broken. If they have been, don't worry too much, just make sure that there are no broken pieces left in the mouth and feed your pet on soft foods such as bread and milk and grated carrots for a week or two and you will find that the teeth will have regrown.

General care Remember that guinea pigs are quite small and can easily be frightened, sometimes to the point of death, so keep dogs and cats well away from them so that they cannot play with them or scare them while they are in their hutches or runs. Finally, do remember that if you go away on holiday for more than a day you must make sure that your guinea pig is well cared for by someone who knows what to feed him and how often.

Check your guinea pig's teeth occasionally to make sure they are sound.

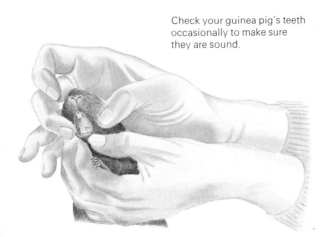

Health and ailments

Occasionally injuries or illness can occur, even in a well cared-for guinea pig, and many of these can be treated by you, though in the case of severe illness guinea pigs seem to lose the will to live very quickly.

The most likely injury to a guinea pig is broken teeth (see page 22), but a similar problem can be that of overgrown back teeth. These teeth are situated right back in the cheeks and cannot be seen, but sometimes overgrow causing the guinea pig difficulty in eating. If

Your guinea pig has grinding teeth at the back of his mouth and incisors at the front.

your pet loses weight and drops partially chewed food instead of eating it then this is the probable cause. Unfortunately the outlook is poor as although your vet may be able to help, the teeth will probably grow back again quickly.

Guinea pigs rarely attack each other, but if two adult males get together they may have a serious fight. When trying to separate fighting guinea pigs you may be bitten, so put on thick gloves, or separate them with a thin sheet of wood and, unless they have serious wounds that need the help of a vet, just clean the bites with weak antiseptic.

Sometimes your pet may get a piece of hay seed in his eye, or may poke it on a stalk. The eye will turn a milky white, but this will usually clear quickly if you make sure there is nothing left in the eye to irritate it and then treat it with a terramycin ointment from your vet.

If your hay contains thistles do try to remove them as they may cause your guinea pig to develop an abscess or large swelling on his throat. This will need veterinary help in opening and cleaning it.

Skin trouble Probably the most common problem among guinea pigs is that of skin trouble, which is usually caused by a tiny mite burrowing under the skin and producing severe irritation. The animal will scratch frantically and lose its fur, particularly on the shoulders and stomach.

It is easily treated, but if left alone the guinea pig will die, as the itching becomes more intense and stress will cause its heart to fail. The best treatment is a dip in a weak solution of Tetmosol, an I.C.I. product, but do *not* follow the instructions with the bottle as these are for human treatment and your guinea pig's skin is very sensitive. Dilute one part of Tetmosol with sixty parts of warm water and dip your pet into a bowl of the mixture, making sure that it soaks down to the skin, then wrap the animal in a warm towel and let it dry naturally. You may have to repeat this procedure after a fortnight or so.

Pneumonia If your guinea pig sits in a hunched-up position and has fast, noisy breathing it probably has pneumonia and the best treatment is warmth and a supply of fluids, perhaps glucose and water given with a dropper.

Your vet may be able to help you by giving your guinea pig tetracycline or a similar medicine, but while terramycins are relatively safe for guinea pigs it is vitally

If your guinea pig scratches and loses weight he may have a skin problem.

A guinea pig being dipped in a weak solution of Tetmosol.

important to remember that they are allergic to penicillin and if given it will usually die.

Diarrhoea This usually means that your guinea pig has eaten something that has disagreed with it and it is best to keep him warm in a really clean box and give him small amounts of a baby's diarrhoea mixture.

However, despite these various problems, guinea pigs are healthy creatures if they are well looked after and not subjected to excessive stress. Remember, their health depends on you, the better you look after them the fitter they will be.

Breeding guinea pigs

Despite popular belief, guinea pigs do not breed at a rapid rate, and are perhaps the slowest breeders of all the small domestic mammals. They are often slow to mate, with a long gestation period of 65-70 days. An average litter will usually be of 2-4 youngsters and these will be born fully furred and with their eyes open. You will find them walking around the cage at an hour old and trying solid food at a day old. The sow usually suckles the young for about three weeks and they can be separated from their mother at four weeks, after which there is a risk of the young males (boars) mating their sisters.

A female guinea pig (a sow) can first be mated as early as 12 weeks of age, and should be retired from breeding at the age of 18-24 months, although older females have successfully had litters.

Guinea pigs are easy to sex, just turn them over and have a look!

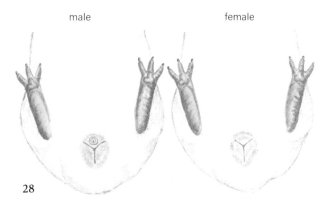

male   female

Young guinea pigs are very precocious, and are tiny replicas of their parents when born.

A sow's pregnancy will be obvious during the latter weeks and it is best to handle her as little as possible and to increase her diet to ensure strong youngsters. It is wise to take the boar away from the sow before the birth, because although he will not harm the babies in any way he will almost certainly mate the sow immediately after the birth, and it is not in the sow's best interests to be suckling one litter whilst carrying the next.

It is easy to determine the sex of your guinea pigs even at an early age, and there is no need to press or squeeze the animal, as with rabbits. Indeed, you may injure your pet if you do this.

Finally, before breeding your guinea pigs, do please bear in mind that you will have to find homes for the youngsters, so make sure that this will not be a problem.

29

Showing

People who show or breed guinea pigs usually refer to them as cavies. Most people who show cavies originally started with a pet, and you too may decide that you would like to exhibit pure-bred cavies. The best thing to do is go along to your local show and look around before deciding which variety you would like to keep. You will find that experienced fanciers (as exhibitors are called) will be pleased to help you, particularly as a show schedule may need a little explanation at first. After deciding to enter your cavy, find out whether you enter in advance or at the show. Then, making sure that your cavy is clean and fit, take him to the show in a sturdy, well ventilated box. When you have entered your cavy you will be given a self-adhesive label with a number on it. Stick this on the outside of your cavy's ear, find the show cage with the same number and put your cavy in it with some bedding.

When the show starts the judge's stewards will fetch the cavies for their classes and bring them to him so that he can examine them. You will learn a lot by watching a judge at work, but don't get in the way and never indicate which cavy is yours. When the judge has finished the stewards will return the cavies and the prize cards will be put on their pens. After judging, take any prize cards your cavy has won to the secretary for your prize money, and then you can take your cavy home.

ADDRESSES
The Secretary, National Cavy Club, 9 Parkdale Road, Sheldon, Birmingham, West Midlands B26 3UT.
The Royal Society for the Prevention of Cruelty to Animals, Causeway, Horsham, Sussex RH12 1HG.
PUBLICATIONS
Cavy World, 20 Wesley Street, Farsley, Pudsey, West Yorkshire. (Available by post only.)

The judge examines each guinea pig thoroughly before deciding on the winner.

Index